# LIMERICKS

D0418157

821.
91
PAL

# LIMERICKS

## Michael Palin

*Illustrated by Tony Ross*

A Red Fox Book

Published by Random House Children's Books
20 Vauxhall Bridge Road, London SW1V 2SA

A division of Random House UK Ltd

London Melbourne Sydney Auckland
Johannesburg and agencies throughout
the world

First published by Hutchinson Children's Books 1985
Beaver edition 1986
Red Fox edition 1992

7 9 10 8 6

Text © Michael Palin 1985
Illustrations © Tony Ross 1985

This book is sold subject to the condition that it shall
not, by way of trade or otherwise, be lent, resold, hired
out, or otherwise circulated without the publisher's
prior consent in any form of binding or cover other
than that in which it is published and without a
similar condition including this condition being im-
posed on the subsequent purchaser

Printed and bound in Great Britain by
Cox & Wyman Ltd, Reading, Berkshire

RANDOM HOUSE UK Limited Reg. No. 954009

Papers used by Random House UK Limited
are natural, recyclable products made from wood grown in
sustainable forests. The manufacturing processes conform to
the environmental regulations of the country of origin

ISBN 0 09 947680 0

# LIMERICKS

## A Foreword By
### *Brigadier Sir Arthur Gumby*

I well remember my days in the Limericks. A finer body of men you could never hope to find. If ever a really difficult task had to be done the Limericks would be called on. Mind you, not all the boys were from Limerick itself. There was a young fellow from Crewe who, as I recall, never knew quite what to do, and there were two colour-sergeants from Rhyl who, as far as I know, are there still, but on the whole they were local boys, born and brought up by the waters of the Shannon. The finest tribute I can pay to these chaps is quite simply to say that when there was a fight and things really got tight, you'd not catch them running away. Such a book is quite long overdue and I hope that you'll all think so too, as it could be, I know, the last chance to show what the Limericks really could do.

A. J. Gumby (Brig. ret.)
Rest Home for the
Partially Deaf, Kuwait

# AUTHOR'S NOTE

There is no easy way to write limericks. The age-old formula of standing in a bucket of Mersey water with a kilt worn inside out is still the best method. There are those who swear by electrodes taped to the head and others who think that carrots eaten from the thick end downwards on the third Sunday of any month with an 's' in it are most effective, but for me there's nothing to beat good hard standing in a bucket.

I have sadly had to abandon certain limericks such as the one about the fellow from Grantham called Titus who was

*A boon to all limerick writers,*
*The number of times*
*His name could make rhymes*
*Was practically ad infinitus,*

on the grounds of being untrue and bad Latin; and the young man from Vermont

*Who had all that a young man could want*
*Nice clothes, lots of cash,*
*A non-serious rash,*
*Except both legs were on back to front,*

as it didn't rhyme; and the policeman from Tring

*Who had an extraordinary thing*

for obvious reasons. And if you can think what to do with the vicar from Usk, whose wife had an elephant's tusk, I'd be very glad to hear about it. Meanwhile, I'd like to thank Caroline Roberts at Hutchinson for helping at times with difficult rhymes and my wife Helen for being subjected to 'how about this?' for six months and still managing to laugh.

A lady musician called Hamp
Was prone to quite severe cramp.
One day at the harp
She got stuck in F-sharp,
And was freed by acetylene lamp.

A chair-lift attendant called Frank
Ate tropical fish from a tank.
When he'd swallowed them whole,
He picked up a bowl
Of goldfish beside them, and drank.

A brave taxi driver called Clive,
Once found a Black Mamba alive.
Though they said, 'Shoot it dead!'
He decided instead
To take it round town for a drive.

A Frenchman called Didier Brume
Had a clear premonition of doom.
So, to hasten his death,
He just held his breath,
And lay, all alone, on a tomb.

A deep-water sailor called Rod
Used to dive in and rescue live cod.
He wasn't a fool
Who thought nets were cruel,
But he certainly was pretty odd.

A batsman from Sydney called Fairlie
Hit a very fast ball good and squarely.
A fielder called Reith
Caught the ball in his teeth –
A thing which he did very rarely.

A pretty young lady called Splatt
Was mistaken one day for a cat
By a man called Van Damm
Who made pets into jam –
And now she's spread out rather flat.

A headmaster's son called McNaught
Got a fright of the nastiest sort,
For when cleaning his teeth
He found bits of Keith
And others his father once taught.

A kindly old fellow called Clore
Gave all that he had to the poor;
But, alas and alack,
They would not give it back,
So he's not giving them any more.

There was a young man called O'Toole,
Who, when he saw food, used to drool;
Pizza, mangoes or tripe,
Avocado, when ripe –
Even gruel made his drool form a pool.

A white cocker spaniel from Poole
Had a thing about Peter O'Toole.
When he came on the telly,
He'd roll on his belly
And do funny things to the stool.

There once was a fellow called Keith
Who wore nothing at all underneath.
When asked was this wise
For a man of his size,
He muttered abuse through clenched
    teeth.

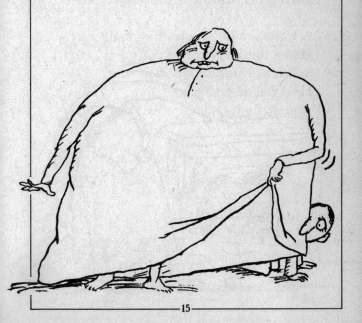

A young man from Grimsby called Short
Used to give things a great deal of thought –
Like, Is there a God?
And, How long's a cod?
And, Is stamp collecting a sport?

A carpenter's helper called Neville
Never made anything level.
A table or chair
Was best made elsewhere,
Then taken to Neville to bevel.

A young man from Redcar, called Vince
Used to drop very obvious hints
Like, 'Oh dear, I *say!*
It's my *birthday* today
And I'm right out of After Eight Mints.'

A lady from Florence called Nella
Had a dog that was such a good smeller
It could sniff out a meal
From as far off as Lille,
And if it was nice it would tell her.

There once was a man called O'Brien
Who, whatever he did, kept his tie on:
In the shower, or deck chair,
He was heard to declare
That 'It shows I'm a man to rely on!'

A javelin thrower called Vicky
Found the grip of her javelin sticky.
When it came to the throw
She just couldn't let go –
Making judging the distance quite tricky.

A very light sleeper called Lowndes
Would wake at the slightest of sounds,
Like a fish thinking hard,
Or the rustling of lard,
Or moles far beneath football grounds.

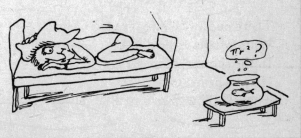

A fellow from Bristol, called Neve,
Was seriously known to believe
That, the world being flat,
If once lost, your cat
Would be terribly hard to retrieve.

A nervous young lady called Hughes
Never knew quite what to choose.
The harder she'd try
The less she knew why,
Or whether, and if so, then whose?

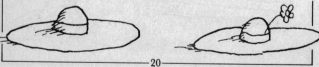

A surgeon from Glasgow called Mac,
Once forgot to put everything back.
As his train made to start,
His case came apart,
And a kidney rolled down off the rack.

There once was a fellow called Scaggs,
Who kept all his things in black bags.
When people asked why,
He'd admit, with a sigh,
There were certainly all sorts of snags.

There was a gravedigger from Barnes
Whose clothes were all covered in darns.
He'd dug fewer holes
In his life, for poor souls,
Than his sweater had under the arms.

A handsome young fellow called Lance
Had over a hundred Great-Aunts.
He kept some in drawers
And some under floors,
And the judge never gave him a chance.

There once was a vicar from Bude
Whose manners at table were rude.
It wasn't the noise,
As he ate saveloys,
But the way that he sat on his food.

An Ilford dog-trainer called Mellish
Made a miniature poodle's life hellish.
It was thought well deserved,
When a dog so reserved
One night ate him, with evident relish.

An impetuous Welshman called Caine
Threw some half-eaten fish from a train.
It struck an MP
Which, I'm sure you'll agree,
Showed a truly impeccable aim.


There once was a man from Malaya
Who refused to pay his bus fare
              (pronounced *fay-er*)
On account of the fact
That the downstairs was packed
And the upstairs reserved for the Mayor.
              (pronounced *may-er*)

*(The author would like to thank the reader for his help with this limerick)*

There was a fishmonger from Leeds
Whose children were all complete weeds –
The sight of a cod
Or anything odd
Would make them go weak at the kneeds.

There once was a man from Dubai,
And to this day no one knows why
He stood on his head,
Slowly spun round, and said,
'EeDiggity Obleson Rye!'

There was a young fellow from Wapping
Who found two live slugs in his shopping.
The girl at the till
Took them both off the bill,
And went on to the next without stopping.


There was a young fellow called Pringle
Who desperately wished to stay single.
But as soon as he saw
One young lady, or more,
He was filled with a strong urge to mingle.

A lady from near Milton Keynes
Had trouble digesting her greens.
The odd Brussels sprout
Would find its way out,
But the greens that bought screams
    were French beans.

There once was a fellow called West
Who found it quite hard to get dressed.
He used to quite dread
Putting socks on his head
And getting both legs through his vest.

A nervous young woman called Fay
Always used to react with dismay
At a match being struck,
Or the quack of a duck.
'Hello, Fay!' made her faint clean away.

A young shipping clerk from Port Said
Was found with his arms and legs tied,
Inside an old trunk
That belonged to a monk
To whom, for advice, he'd applied.

There once was a man from Manila
Who christened his young son Attila.
It was only in fun –
But he grew up a Hun,
Renowned through the world as a killer.

There was a young fellow from Malta,
Who bought his grandfather an altar,
But, as happens to most,
It broke in the post,
As it squeezed through the Straits of
    Gibraltar.

A singer related to Brahms
Showed an ambulance driver her charms.
He liked them so much
He allowed her to touch
The knob that set off the alarms.

A young man from Utah, called Paul
Had a head several sizes too small,
For the price of a dollar
He'd loosen his collar
And show how far down it could fall.

There once was a camper called Jack
Who found a huge snake in his pack.
He cut it in two,
Gave half to the zoo,
And then put the other half back.

A man from the north, called Adair,
When he washed, never took proper care:
At first it was spots,
Then rashes, then lots
Of patches of unwanted hair.

An arm-wrestling vicar from Looe
Invited some friends to a do.
Dressed only in shorts,
He taught them some sports
They thought very few vicars knew.

A young mountaineer called Vic
Became quite close friends with a stick.
He took it for walks,
And they had little talks,
Then it left him to live with a brick.

A young discus-thrower called Earl
Could not take his eyes off a girl,
Which is rather bad luck –
With them hopelessly stuck
He can no longer see where to hurl.

There once was a fellow called Maude
Who became very easily bored,
One day, at a lunch,
He fell in a bunch
Of lupins, and lay there, ignored.

There was a young fellow called Lloyd
Who everyone tried to avoid.
It wasn't the smell,
Or the stories he'd tell,
But the way he pronounced Bettws-y-coed.

(Author's note: *This limerick will work best for experienced Welsh speakers.*)

There was a young man from Kashmir
Who shouted, one day, 'Over here!'
But from so far away
That he's still there today,
And will be for ever, I fear.

A curious fellow called Stoat
Bought jewellery and things for a goat.
For favours like these
It gave milk and cheese
And kicked him one day in the throat.

A young man from Berwick-on-Tweed
Kept a very strange thing on a lead.
He was never once seen
To give it a clean
Or anything else it might need.

A peculiar fellow called Long
Once sat on a very sharp prong.
He gave a great shout –
As his friends pulled it out.
Then he sat on the next one along.

There once was a tortoise called Joe
Whose progress was painfully slow.
He'd stop for a week,
Look around, take a peek,
Then, unlike a shot, off he'd go.

A man by the name of Geneen
Was asked by his wife where he'd been.
He *Ummed* and he *Ahhhhed* –
So she hit him, quite hard,
On the head, with a large soup tureen.

A young scuba-diver called Jeff
Was so good at holding his breff
He could swim anywhere
On a lungful of air
Which scared his poor muvver to deff.


A handsome young fellow called Miles
Used to help pretty girls over stiles.
Once over the top
One or two used to stop,
But the rest kept on going for Miles.

An excitable fellow called Gomez
Told his dog 'I don' wanna *no* mess.
Cleaning the floor
I ain't doin' no more,
And I've had it with nasty aromas.'

A handsome young fellow called Frears
Was attracted to girls by their ears.
He'd traverse the globe
For a really nice lobe,
And the sight would reduce him to tears.

A curious lady called Davies
Used to make threatening phone calls
   to Avis.
She'd pretend to be mad,
And ask if they had
Any cars called Lucinda or Mavis.


A mother from Seascale called Pippa
Found some nuclear waste in a kipper.
When she told them she'd found it,
They said, 'Eat around it,
And keep it away from the nipper.'

A Sussex fast bowler called Lyall
Took a run-up of nearly a mile.
In one Gillette Cup
He never turned up –
And was last seen just south of the Nile.

A curious young man from Calcutta,
Was known as a bit of a nutter.
After prawn vindaloo
And a Guinness or two
He'd lie, very still, in the gutter.

A South African farmer called Ted
Attacked a brick wall with his head.
The blow could be felt,
All over the veldt,
And in less than an hour he was dead.


There was a young lady called Marge
Who liked men with features quite large.
Her long line of suitors
Had whacking great hooters,
Apart from a Monsieur Lafarge.

An hotelier, name of O'Rourke
Once had a quail that could talk.
It would make little nests,
And shout at the guests,
And warn against eating the pork.

An optician who practised in Rye
Sadly had only one eye.
He'd given the other
To somebody's brother,
And it wasn't the thing to ask why.

There was a young fellow called Priestley,
Whose behaviour to women was beastly.
He'd promise them wine
And a jolly good time –
Then give them a weekend in Eastleigh.


A cartoonist from Worksop, called Botts
Tied himself in such intricate knots
That even his friends
Could not find the ends,
And he died, still unravelled, in Notts.

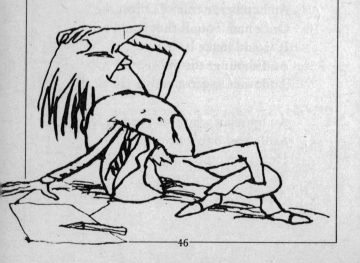

One day in a small town on Skye
A finger turned up in a pie,
Then a nose and two lips,
Then a fine pair of hips,
Then a waitress jumped out and said, 'Hi!'

## The Penarth Double Limerick

A fisherman's wife from Penarth
Invented a new way to laugh,
Using both of her feet
And a long rubber sheet
Which her son folded neatly in half.

When she felt a good joke coming on,
She'd shout, 'Get the rubber sheet, John!'
But when it was found
And laid out on the ground
Whatever was funny had gone.

An ageing shot-putter called Carl
Used to pull back his lips in a snarl,
Revealing, beneath,
Several rows of white teeth
And a bridge he'd had fitted in Arles.

There was a surveyor from Kent
Whose theodolite got rather bent.
The result you can see
On the A423,
Which never goes quite where they meant.

A lodger from Brighton called Briggs
Had a penchant for syrup of figs;
Though he did what he could,
The results were so good
He had to keep moving his digs.

A young ballet dancer called Bruce
Wore tights that were rather too loose.
As he leapt through the air
All his skills were laid bare,
And his face went a very bright puce.

A highly-strung lady called Weems,
Once caught a man in her dreams.
He vanished away
In the cold light of day –
But he left her some peppermint creams.

A refuse collector called Bert
Had a priceless collection of dirt
Covered up by a screen
To keep it all clean,
With a guard dog on constant alert.

A chiropodist – friends call her Dawn –
Used to do people's feet on her lawn;
But the neighbours complained
When a lady, unnamed,
Was hit in the eye by a corn.

A jolly old fellow called Boakes
Knew five thousand eight hundred jokes,
Which, ranging from bad
To the dismally sad,
He tried out on helpless old folks.

A greedy young fellow called Wrench
Owned a cat, two small dogs, and a tench.
One day, in a trice,
He cooked them with rice,
And called the dish something in French.

A curious fellow called Lamb
Used to shout things at old tins of Spam
Like, 'You silly old tin!'
And, 'Where have *you* been?'
Then he'd move on and rubbish the jam.

A trainee magician called Mick
Made a frightful mistake with a trick,
When he turned a small boy,
His mum's pride and joy,
Irreversibly into a brick.

A Wrexham tattooist called Ken
Used to draw little pictures on men;
Sometimes a still life,
Or another man's wife,
Or, once in a while, Tony Benn.

There was a young fellow called Clem
Who possessed quite remarkable phlegm:
When he once by mistake
Choked to death on a cake,
He got up and did it again.

There was a young fellow called Grist
Who found the girls hard to resist.
He'd give them the eye,
But was so deeply shy
That he always just missed being kissed.

A veterinary surgeon from Fife
Once dressed up to frighten his wife.
When asked, 'Is it wise?'
He replied in surprise,
'Where I come from this sort of thing's rife.'

There once was a poet called Sime
Who avoided the obvious rhyme.
He'd put 'this' after 'that',
And 'dog' after 'cat',
And he hated this sort of last line.

A lady from Louth with a lisp
Liked her sausages specially crisp.
But in trying to say
That she liked them that way
She covered her friends in a mitht.

There once was a fellow called Doyle
Who covered up people with soil
Long before they were dead –
Which would make them see red,
And bring quite placid chaps to the boil.

A gravedigger's helper called Maddox
Was obsessed with an urge to ride haddocks.
He made little paddles,
And waterproof saddles,
But the fish never stayed in the paddocks.

An earnest young lady called Soames
Wrote a very large book about gnomes;
But the tales were so tall
And the sales were so small
She was left with huge unwanted tomes.

A lady from Brighton called Palmer
Became quite an expert snake charmer.
The snakes called her Miss,
And gave a loud hiss
When it looked as if someone would
     harm her.

A research biochemist from Goring
Found cricketers rather alluring.
He'd turn up at the match
And hope for a catch
Or something a bit more enduring.

A Yorkshireman living in Worcester
Said to his wife, 'Fetch a duster.
This table from Hull
Has gone ever so dull.
A duster will bring back its lustre.'

*(To be read only in a Yorkshire accent.)*

A lady from Bristol called Bligh,
Who all of her life had been shy,
Was cured in a week
By two Poles and a Greek
Whom she met on the Island of Skye.

An unemployed dentist called Hodge
Rolled used cotton wool in a wodge,
Which he fired, with some force,
From the back of a horse,
Causing elderly people to dodge.

A travelling salesman called Lloyd
Was known as a man to avoid.
The horrified stares
As he showed off his wares
Was a sight that he clearly enjoyed.

A fisherman living in York
Complained that the length of the walk
From his house to the sea
Took two days or three,
And more if he stopped for a talk.

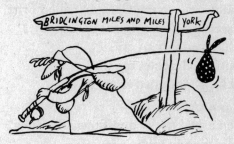

A butcher's assistant called Phil
Was caught with his hands in the till.
He tried to cut meat
Using only his feet
But the sight made the customers ill.

A handsome young German called Fritz,
On seeing a friend do the splits,
With a triumphant cry,
Shouted, 'Here, let me try!'
And broke into two equal bits.

When asked tricky questions, old Riley
Would simply reply, very drily,
'I'm sorry, old bean,
I don't know what you mean,'
Then sidle off home, smiling wryly.

A dog from Sri Lanka called Patch
Sat down on a tree stump to scratch;
But he found that the flea,
Was not one, but three,
And the first of a very large batch.

A man called O'Hara one day
Decided he'd make the world pay.
He wrote down a plan
To destroy every man –
But the wind came and blew it away.

There was a young man from Melrose
Who had a large thing on his nose,
One on his back,
And three in a sack,
And four between each of his toes.


A young man from Beccles, called Duke,
Discovered one day, by a fluke,
If he put on a fez
And a little pince-nez
He looked like the young King Farouk.

A man from Bloemfontein – a Boer –
Was awfully hard to ignore.
He'd see you and shout,
'Let's have a meal out!'
Unless you were coloured, or poor.

A Tory backbencher called Sandys
Detested the sound of brass bandys.
When they started to play
He'd run far away,
And cover his head with his handys.

(Author's note: *Ask an aged relative how to pronounce 'Sandys'.*)

There was a young fellow called Ben,
Who angered his friends now and then
By running up stairs
And shouting, 'Who cares?'
Then doing the whole thing again.

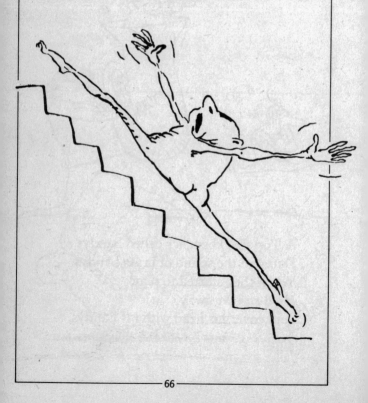

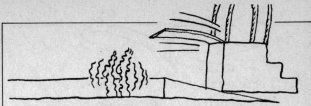

A strange man called Ron took a bet:
He'd swim three lengths without getting wet.
With commendable cool
He emptied the pool,
Dived in, and has not come round yet.

There was a young fellow called Owen
Who had to keep goin' and goin'.
Psychiatrists said
Being dropped on his head
Had caused all the toin' and froin'.

A girl from Carlisle called Lucy
One day came over all goosy.
Although it seemed strange,
She got used to the change,
And by Christmas was really quite juicy.

A boxer from Malta called Raymon
Used a big concrete wall to take aim on.
He broke both his arms
And three lucky charms –
One with his grandmother's name on.

A vicar from Esher called Hughes
Used to greatly enjoy a quick snooze
At lunchtime, or tea
If the pulpit was free,
And if not, he'd kip in the pews.

There once was a fellow called God,
Whom everyone thought rather odd.
Apart from a lady
Called Eileen O'Grady,
Who worshipped the ground that he trod.

An aspiring young MP from Tring
Invented a very neat thing.
He created a voter,
Complete with a motor,
Which he found would support anything.

A curious fellow named Kurt
Used to climb Alpine peaks in a skirt.
He said it felt nice
In the snow and the ice,
And it kept those below more alert.

A curious man named McGraw
Caught part of his head in a door.
When he came back next week
With his wife, who was Greek,
He found it, still there, on the floor.

An elderly lady from Fleet
Once scored a goal with both feet,
And, despite her great age,
Earns a reasonable wage
As reserve centre forward for Crete.

There once was a lady called Tate
Who won a live bear at a fete.
To her home it was led,
But it hadn't been fed,
And the police got there seconds too late.


There was a young fellow called Kamp
Who sunbathed in his loo with a lamp.
But a flash in the pan
Gave him more than a tan –
The result of the wires getting damp.

A retired metal-worker called Noades
Used to solve little problems for toads,
Like where to jump next,
Or a hard Latin text,
Or how to avoid major roads.

There was a young man from the Cape
Who swallowed his hat for a jape.
It was easy to tell
Why he felt so unwell
By his stomach's extraordinary shape.

There once was a teacher called Fox,
Who kept something rare in a box.
One night, as dawn broke,
The creature awoke
And ran off with his shoes and his socks.

A very smart lady from Rye
Had an accent that gave her awye.
She said she was posh,
Which they all knew was tosh –
She came from East Ham, so they sye.


A young mountaineer from Nepal
Invented a new way to fall.
It worked out so well
That no one could tell
Where he was – if he'd landed at all.

There once was a young man called Potter,
Whose girlfriend resembled an otter –
About three feet long,
Smooth brown fur, fairly strong:
No one quite liked to ask where he'd got her.

There was a young lady called Ben
Who got on ever so well with the men.
It wasn't the beard
Or the way that she cheered
But the pipe that she smoked now and then.

A man on a length of elastic
Decided to do something drastic.
When he jumped off the cliff he
Came back in a jiffy,
And screamed to his friends, 'It's fantastic!'